GARDENING
A Useful Alphabet

GARDENING
A Useful Alphabet

❧

ANNA
PAVORD

with wood engravings by

YVONNE
SKARGON

COLT BOOKS
Cambridge

Colt Books Ltd
9 Clarendon Road
Cambridge, CB2 2BH
Tel:(01223) 329059   Fax:(01223) 65866

First published by Colt Books 1995

ISBN 0 905899 16 4

British Library Cataloguing-in-Publication Data
A catalogue record for this book is available from the British Library

Design by Clare Byatt

Printed in Great Britain by Biddles Ltd, Guildford.

Acid or Alkaline

This is a term that applies to soil which is acid, alkaline or, if you are lucky, neutral. There are kits like toy chemistry sets to tell you what soil you have. Measurement is by pH (potential of hydrogen). The scale runs from 1 to 14. Neutral is around 7. Above that, soils are said to be alkaline, below it, acid. Most vegetables grow best in a slightly alkaline soil. Rhododendrons need acid soil, between 4·5 and 6 on the pH scale. Happy gardeners work with what they have got and grow plants that like their soil. There is nothing more miserable than a miserable rhododendron, panting for its acid fix in a sea of lime. (*See also* pH.)

nnual

Larkspur, love-in-a-mist, sunflower, pot marigold are all annuals, completing their whole life cycle from seed to seed in a single season. Sow them in spring, pull them up in autumn. Use them for patches of colour to fill in between more permanent plants. Essential for the authentic cottage garden look. (*See also* Bedding Plants.)

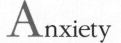nxiety

Novice gardeners worry too much. Relax. Gardening is supposed to be an enjoyment, not a rite of passage. Plants are programmed to survive and will do their best to overcome whatever crass things you do to them. Remember, experts always make things more complicated than they need be. It is a form of self-protection. The simplest way to happiness is to mark down what does well in your garden and then grow a lot of it.

Apple

Every garden should have one, but not a Cox
which is one of the most difficult apples to grow
well. It gets sick easily (scab is one of its diseases)
which means too much spraying. Visit the
Brogdale Horticultural Trust orchards at Faversham
in Kent for apple tastings and advice on the best
varieties to grow in your particular area. Pruning
enhances performance, but apples will bear perfectly adequately without it. Keep a clear circle of
earth round their trunks, free of grass or other
competitors. Help the tree to grow, before fussing
about its pruning.

Bedding Plants

These are invaluable, especially in bare, new gardens. Resist the temptation to buy them too early. They cannot survive frosts. In London gardens, warmed by escaped central heating, you can risk setting out bedding plants from the beginning of May. Anywhere else, wait until the end of the month. Although it is difficult to resist, do not buy plants already in flower. They will not settle so easily nor last so long as plants that have put their efforts into establishing good roots. Avoid plants that have yellowed leaves. Good bedding plants should be compact, stocky and growing in moist soil. (*See also* Annuals.)

Biennial

This is a plant that needs two growing seasons to fulfil its life cycle. During the first year, it grows a rosette of leaves. During the second, it flowers and sets seed. In a small garden, you may not feel like tying up ground that long before there is any action. It is worth it. Foxgloves, evening primroses, honesty, some verbascums are biennials. All are generous self seeders, so once you have introduced a biennial to the garden, you will not have to do anything about keeping it there.

Blanching

Something that only vegetable gardeners need to know about. The word comes from the French and it means to make something whiter. The effect of this is to make whatever it is you are blanching more succulent as well, because it is forced to grow faster than it would normally do. You blanch vegetables by covering them up, excluding light, and it is usually done to crops such as celery or chicory. The method of blanching depends on the vegetable. With celery you tie paper collars round the plants and heap earth around them so the stems are well buried. Chicory is usually forced inside a shed or greenhouse, and covered with pots or boxes.

Bulb

Like an egg, the perfectly designed package. If you cut one down the middle, you will find pale fleshy leaves, modified versions of the ones above ground, wrapped tightly round an embryo flower. Bulbs nearly always work the first season, thanks to the efficient Dutch producers. Some then give up, which may mean you have not given them what they need to initiate the next embryo bud. Or they may have been eaten by mice. Or pheasants. Or squirrels. Bulbs are popular.

Buying

In spring it is impossible to resist the call of the nursery and garden centre. Blinded by an optimism of the most irrational kind, you ricochet from plant to plant, each one the centre of a new dream. Resist the temptation to pick up only those plants that are in flower at the time. They will not settle as easily as a plant that has had time to think about its roots before it has to worry about what's going on above.

We are lucky in Britain to have a network of brilliant specialist nurseries, many of whom will send plants by mail order. Look for them in *The Plant Finder* (Headmain). There is an increasing trend to sell expensive big plants (especially herbaceous perennials) rather than cheaper small ones. If you are on a strict budget, buy small and be patient. Herbaceous perennials will catch up quickly. Look for sale bargains among slow growing plants such as magnolia, camellia, holly. A well-grown plant of one of these may save you five years of waiting.

Check whether a plant is root bound or has been hastily repotted, by slipping it out of its pot before you buy. If there is a matted coil of roots twirling round like spaghetti, don't waste cash on it. It may have difficulty kicking the habit of circular growth and may never get itself securely anchored in the ground.

Chlorosis

A problem which turns leaves that should be bright pulsating green a pallid, sickly yellow. It happens when the plant cannot absorb the minerals it needs from the soil. Minerals make chlorophyll. Chlorophyll makes green. A dose of iron (ask your ironmonger) often helps.

Cold Frame

A doll's greenhouse, unheated as the name suggests and built low, with a sloping glass roof which you slide on and off depending on the weather. The warmest type has a brick rather than a glass base. Use it to harden off (*qv*) plants that you have raised from seed. (*See also* Greenhouse.)

Compost

This has two different meanings. When bought in a sack, it applies to the stuff you fill your seed trays with. This sort of compost is made from loam (good fertile soil), from peat (which we are not now supposed to use) or some peat substitute such as coir.

The other sort of compost is the stuff you have stacked in a bin or a heap in the farthest corner of the garden. Any organic material — vegetable peelings, weeds, grass mowings, leaves, dead birds — can go into a compost heap. Hair is excellent, full of minerals that plants need, though only in minute quantities. Gradually, the whole lot rots down into something that looks very much like earth, but is generally called humus. Nettles are useful on compost heaps as they speed up the rate of decomposition. Covering the heap with old carpet also helps.

Compost is good for the garden. It helps things to grow by providing food and it helps the soil by improving its structure. Light soils get heavier, better at hanging on to moisture, when you add compost to them. Heavy soils get lighter as the compost creates air spaces round the particles of clay. (*See also* Humus, Leafmould, Mulching.)

Conifer

So called because they carry their seeds in cones. Their leaves are thin and needle like (as in pines and cypress trees) and they are usually evergreen. The odd man out is larch. It is a conifer but it drops its leaves in autumn.

Cuttings

Once you start thinking about cuttings you are no longer a beginner. You will buy a book such as Peter Thompson's *Creative Propagation* and bore on at dinner parties about the best way to strike *Daphne bholua*. Propagation can easily become an obsession. There is no more wildly parental feeling than watching your first successful cutting turn into a grown-up bush.

Start with geraniums. They are least likely to let you down, are always useful and are expensive to buy. You need to look for bushy new shoots without flowers. They will have stems of bright green, rather than the woody, buff colour of old geranium stems. The reason for choosing shoots without flowers is that you want your cutting to put all its effort into producing roots, without having to bother about what is happening on top.

Choose cuttings about three or four inches long and make the cut just below a leaf joint. Strip off all the lowest leaves, leaving the cutting only with a topknot of small immature leaves. Geranium cuttings will root in water, but it saves trouble if you stick them immediately into a mixture in which they can settle.

Tender new roots do not want immediately to be bashing their noses against impenetrable particles of soil. The aim of any good cuttings mixture is that it should be easy for roots to infiltrate. A mixture of peat and sand is the traditional medium. Vermiculite and compost is just as good. Vermiculite is an absorbent, lightweight granular substance made from a mineral rather like mica.

Some cuttings need to be covered with a plastic bag, rooting most easily in a moist, enclosed atmosphere. Geranium cuttings do not. Stand the pot in a light, airy place, free from frost and keep it moist, but not sopping.

You can take geranium cuttings at any time, but in terms of having decent plants to set outside in May, September is the most effective month. You can then bulk the plants up over winter. March is also good, but this depends on your having somewhere to overwinter the mother plants so that they can be raided for cuttings in spring.

If you go for the March method, you need to force the overwintered plants into growth so that they will provide plenty of juicy new cuttings. Do this by cutting back the old plant, watering and feeding it generously six weeks before. Cuttings should root in ten days.

Damping Down

Only those with greenhouses have to do this. It is a way of keeping the air inside the greenhouses moistly humid, which is what makes plants purr and red spider, an insect pest, cough. Do it in hot weather by hosing down the floor frequently with cold water.

Danger

This will be as nothing compared with the dangers we encounter daily when driving a car. The biggest dangers are likely to come from machinery which is a good reason for having as little as possible.

Beware of taking over a greenhouse wired up for heat by an amateur electrician. Learn everything you need to know about trip switches and power breakers. Beware the sharp end of canes. Use slug pellets cautiously if there are dogs and children in the house. Use poisonous chemicals as sparingly as possible.

Deadheading

Where and when to cut are the most pressing questions for the novice gardener. Take geraniums: do you nip off each individual floret as it fades in the head or do you wait for the whole head to go to seed before you cut the flower stem off where it joins the main stem? Either is good. Time is the deciding factor. It had never occurred to me to do the former until an anxious beginner enquired whether he was doing the Right Thing.

A plant's main purpose is to perpetuate itself by producing seeds. Deadheading forces many of them to produce more and more flowers in a desperate effort to fulfil their biological destiny. Some respond better than others.

Roses are always worth deadheading. Find the point at which the flower stem joins a bigger stem and make your cut just above the first outward facing bud after that junction. This is counsel of perfection. Some roses have excellent hips and the later flush of flowers should be left so that you have something to look forward to in autumn.

Annual flowers also respond well to regular deadheading. You will notice this particularly with ageratum, antirrhinum (snapdragon), calendula (marigold), centaurea (cornflower), cosmos and sweet peas. Violas also need picking over fairly frequently. Use shears to trim over mat-like varieties such as *Viola cornuta*.

Early flowering perennials can sometimes be persuaded to perform again in late summer if you cut them down hard as soon as they have finished flowering. Alchemilla is a case in point. Try this also with campanula, centranthus (valerian), hardy geraniums, helianthemum (rock rose), and oriental poppy. Use shears for carpeters such as the rock rose.

The tidiest way to dead head is to take out the whole of the flowering stem and make the cut as low down as you can. Bulbs are an exception to this rule. Daffodils and tulips are not very leafy. The bulb below ground needs the extra nourishment that is fed back into it by the flower stem. When you are deadheading these, just nip the dead flowers off and leave the stem intact.

Deep Bed System

Unfortunately, not as luxuriously sybaritic as it sounds. This is a way of growing plants, usually vegetables in a series of beds, no more than four to five feet wide. The beds are divided by narrow paths, about a foot wide. This sort of layout means you can do all the planting, weeding and general cultivation from the paths, without ever treading on the beds. This avoids compaction, helps drainage and soil structure and cuts down radically on the digging — unnecessary when the beds are established. Heavy mulching is the norm and so the beds tend to get higher than the paths. That is why they are called deep beds.

What you lose on the pathways, you gain by more intensive cropping in the beds. Plant in short rows running across the beds with plants equidistant from one another. Because you are planting closely, you must feed the soil well. The easiest way is with a bulky organic mulch. The labour of making the beds has so far deterred me from trying this system, but those who have swear by it. It also makes rotation of crops a much simpler proposition.

Digging

Only masochists make this loom large in the gardening calendar. On heavy ground, you dig to expose clods of earth so that they can be broken up by frost. You dig to get air into the soil, to bury weeds or other organic material. You also dig to give robins a decent breakfast.

In the Percy Thrower school of gardening, digging had heroic status, together with bastard trenching and double digging which was twice as back breaking. On light soils, forking over will often be enough. Mushroom compost or any other weed-free compost that you can spread thickly on top of the ground will eventually be pulled down into the earth by worms. This is a lot less trouble than doing it yourself.

If you are creating a new border, it may not be necessary to dig the earth at all. If you garden on light, sandy soil weedkill it thoroughly, mulch it heavily and plant direct into the ground. Heavy ground, or places which have been used as throughways, need more attention. Digging improves drainage and introduces air into earth which has been hard packed by feet.

Heavy clay soils should be dug at the beginning of winter, light soils as late as possible in spring. Light soils do not need to be broken down by frost. The main problem here is hanging on to water and nutrients. By leaving the soil firm over winter, you will be helping it to hold as much water as possible.

Earwigs

These generally get a bad press, which is not entirely fair. They have an unfortunate liking for the flowers of clematis and dahlia. But they are also good predators and can deal effectively with several far worse pests: small caterpillars, aphids and the eggs of codling moths.

Earwigs are most active between May and October. They are night feeders, resting by day in cool dark hidey-holes. The traditional trap is a flowerpot stuffed with straw and stuck upside down on a pole near the war zone. The idea is to empty the flowerpot and its attendant earwigs somewhere far from the scene of the crime.

Other similar traps are equally effective. You can

make rolls of corrugated cardboard or sacking to fix on sticks. Hollow broad bean stalks stuck in the ground also attract earwigs. If you suddenly feel like squashing them, think what exemplary mothers they are. Unusually among insects, they show some interest in the eggs they have laid. If their maternal qualities leave you cold, remember what they are doing to the aphids.

Eelworm

Unlike the earwig, this is a baddy with no redeeming features. Microscopic stem and bulb eelworm infects narcissus, invading the tissue of the bulb and multiplying so rapidly that a million can exist in a single bulb. You will know if you have got it as flowers collapse completely. Burn infected stock and do not replant bulbs in the same place for a while.

Potato eelworm can also be a big problem. These are soil-borne pests that hatch out from eggs protected by a tough brown cyst. The young eel-worms home in on the roots of potato plants. In the worst instances, the whole plant dies. Crop rotation is the best defence. Do not grow maincrop potatoes on the same patch more than once every five years. Some varieties of potato have partial resistance to eelworm. Look for 'Cara', 'Concorde', 'Jewel', 'Maris Piper', 'Morag', 'Penta' and 'Pentland Javelin'.

F_1 Hybrid

You find the term most often used in seed catalogues. The F stands for first generation, a seed strain that has been produced by crossing two closely related varieties of a plant. The plants that you grow from the seed resulting from this cross usually have greater vigour than either the mother or the father. Parents will recognise the scenario.

ertilizers

These are compounds, natural or manufactured, which you use to replace nutrients and restore soil fertility. A bitter argument rages about the benefits of one against the other. Although only green in parts, I prefer natural rather than the other. Using high octane inorganic fertilizers is like using hard drugs. Instant benefit is cancelled out by long-term problems. Only where plants are grown in unnatural circumstances (usually confined spaces such as pots, hanging baskets and the like) are you likely to need manufactured fertilizers.

Leaving aside the global argument against nitrates, leaching, pollution and the rest, think of what they do to your soil. Manufactured fertilizers work fast. That is one of the reasons they are popular. But they feed the plant rather than the soil. This upsets the delicate balance of the soil's own life, which includes important micro-organisms invisible to our eyes. Soil can die. It's just that we cannot see the process. Manufactured fertilizers do not supply as clever a balance of nutrients as the plant can supply for itself, if the

soil is in good heart. Nitrates promote rapid growth, but plants fed in this way grow artificially. They often have too high a water content. They are sappy and more open to attack by pest and disease. Which leads you to reach for a different bottle . . . .

Natural fertilizers supply nutrients of plant or animal origin. Seaweed, hoof and horn, bonemeal are typical. These are broken down by bacteria in the soil and then drawn in by the plants' roots. Neither inorganic nor organic fertilizers are enough on their own. You also need to add bulky manures (compost or farmyard manure) to the soil to enhance fertility and structure.

Fungicide

This can be used to fight against a wide range of common diseases. It can combat powdery mildew, particularly prevalent in hot, dry summers. It will also work against grey mould (botrytis) which attacks strawberries and other plants. Leaf spots, such as black spot on roses may also be controlled with a systemic fungicide.

Fungicides work in different ways. The systemic types are absorbed through the leaves into the sap of the plant, there killing any resident fungus spores. Contact fungicides work by making a barrier between the leaf surface and any hopeful external spores. They will only be efficient if they are applied regularly, usually at ten to fourteen day intervals.

All fungicides are better at prevention than cure. Unfortunately, most gardeners are better at reacting than foretelling. If plants are growing strongly in well-nurtured soil and in the sort of position that nature intended for them, they will be less prone to any kind of disease. This is your best defence.

If spots, blights and other fungi get the upper hand *Gardening Which?* recommend Dithane 945 (pbi) for blackspot on roses, Nimrod-T (ICI) for blackspot and mildew combined, Systhane (pbi) for rose rust and Tumbleblite (Murphy) for rust on other garden plants. For a full account get hold of their *Guide to Pests and Diseases.*

Greenfly

They come with the roses, clustering sometimes so thickly around the buds, that you think the bud is another leaf. Together with the slug, this is the most commonly complained about garden pest. The greenfly is one of the 550 different kinds of aphid that thrive in Britain. They breed prodigiously because for the whole of the summer all aphids are female and their young grow up in a week, and then start to give birth themselves. Don't *think* about it. It is too frightening. Greenfly are sap suckers and virus spreaders. Their enemies are ladybirds and hoverflies. If you spray greenfly *only* use an insecticide (such as ICI's Rapid) that is specific to this particular pest. If you use an all-purpose killer, you will wipe out your friends as well as your foes.

Greenhouse

Extra warmth and shelter for plants are the benefits. This means that you can extend the growing season of all plants and grow tender and tropical plants that would not survive outside in the garden. Unfortunately, greenhouses provide ideal living conditions for pests as well as plants. Be prepared for armies of whitefly and red spider.

Aluminium greenhouses glassed to the ground are the most popular. Although maintenance is minimal and the design allows maximum light to reach the plants, they are cold and condensation can be a greater problem than in wooden greenhouses. But wood, even cedar, needs looking after.

Plastic tunnels seem the most economical alternative, but do not last long. Even polythene sheeting that has been treated against ultraviolet light rarely lasts for more than three years and is easily punctured, or tears in high winds.

Roof ventilators are vital. You need a ventilated area equal to at least twenty per cent of the floor space. Automatic ventilators are essential for anyone who is likely to be frequently away from their greenhouse. They are designed round a cylinder of sensitive wax, which expands or contracts according to the temperature. The cylinder moves a piston rod attached to the ventilator. All automatic ventilators should be marked with the weight they can lift. Check that you have got one that is man enough for the job. You can weigh vent frames by resting kitchen scales under the bottom edge.

Heating will depend on your purse. In any case, arrange the greenhouse so that you can partition off part of it to keep frost free in winter. Electricity is reckoned an expensive option, though installation is relatively cheap. Remember that keeping a greenhouse at a winter temperature of 50°F (10°C) costs twice as much as keeping it at 45°F (7°C). Paraffin heaters are cheap, but not so precise. Insulation is a sensible measure. Use heavy duty bubble polythene fixed with clips to the inside of the greenhouse frame. In very cold areas leave this insulation in place on the north side to provide extra protection and warmth through the summer.

Ground Cover

A catch-all term applied to plants that spread to cover the soil. They protect it and, if they are strong growers, stop weeds from sprouting in the same place. The trick is to choose plants that can outpace weeds but that are not such thugs that they become weeds themselves.

The term is often used in a rather despairing way as though ground cover were some necessary but cheap kind of linoleum. You should not think of it like this. You can turn it into an invaluable carpet. Think of it as the bottom layer of a three-tiered planting plan, contrasting with its own neighbours on the ground floor but also providing a foil for the inhabitants of the upper storeys.

Ground cover does not have supernatural power to suppress weed. Smothering is its technique. When it is established, it is reasonably efficient at keeping down annual weeds. It is powerless against established perennials such as marestail, bindweed and creeping thistle.

Some plants recommended for ground cover, such as periwinkle (*Vinca*) take a long time to achieve sufficient bulk to do their job. Others, such as alchemilla, are over-exuberant colonisers. The big family of geraniums (quite different from the tender summer flowering container plants) are among the best ground cover plants. Bugle (*Ajuga*), lungwort (*Pulmonaria*), London Pride (*Saxifraga x urbium*) all do well in shady positions, provided it is not dry.

Growing Bags

These are heavy duty plastic sacks filled with
compost of the soilless type. They act as instant
gardens. With these, you can grow crops on
balconies, or in yards carpeted with concrete, but
the plants will still need light, air, water and food.
Because they are relatively shallow, growing bags
dry out quickly.

Tomatoes are a favourite crop. The most recent research shows that the best-tasting tomatoes come from plants that have been well fed but kept on the dry side. To avoid problems with staking, use one of the small-fruited bush tomatoes.

Concrete makes a cold base. For sulky plants such as tomatoes that only get going when the soil has warmed up, insulate the bags by slipping some polystyrene tiles under them.

Tomatoes are greedy, so they should have the first turn in the bag. You can use the bags a second time if you choose a less demanding crop such as radish or lettuce. You can also use bags for a permanent crop such as mint, chives or strawberries.

Before replanting, ease out the roots of the previous crop and fork over the compost in the bag. Do not feed the new plants until they are well established. Over feeding causes a build up of unhelpful salts which will eventually retard growth rather than promote it.

French beans are very successful in growing bags. You can get about twelve plants in each. Raise the seeds inside, sown singly in three-inch pots. If you sow at the end of April, the plants should be ready to go in the bags at the end of May.

Half Hardy

The phrase is used in two different contexts, both of which end up meaning the same thing. A half hardy shrub is one that, like acacia, may survive happily outside through the winter in frost-free parts of Cornwall, but will shrivel hideously before your eyes if you ask it to do the same thing in Yorkshire.

Hardiness is a measure of a plant's ability to stand up to cold. Only by experience do you learn what you can get away with. In London, where central heating leaks out by the btu-load, plants that are generally described as half hardy will often overwinter very successfully. The degree of dampness also has an important effect on survival. Some plants will endure a few degrees of frost as long as it is dry.

Half hardy bedding plants are those such as petunia or French marigold that you set out towards the end of May when frost is no longer likely to be a problem. They are the ones that are sold in plastic strips, or which you raise yourself from seed indoors. Hardy annuals can be sown direct outside, either in September to overwinter or in spring.

Hardening Off

By this means, you acclimatise a plant to tougher conditions than it has been used to. You are usually told to do it with seedlings before you plant them out. Seeds are raised in a warm, sheltered environment which makes growth sappy and delicate. Before they are planted outside permanently, you need to give them a sniff of real life. In response, they will gradually adjust to the conditions by toughening their stems and leaves.

You harden off a plant by slowly increasing the length of time you leave it outside. At first, it cannot stay outside at night when temperatures drop markedly. You also need to watch for late frosts. Bedding plants offered for sale in spring should already be hardened off. If plants look drawn or sappy, avoid them.

Herbicide

The essence of gardening is maintaining a balance between the things you want in your garden and those you don't. Weeding is extremely therapeutic, and there is no better way of learning about your plants than being constantly amongst them, refereeing between bindweed and clematis, ground elder and hostas. But herbicides (weedkillers) have their place, too.

The most important distinction between the different sorts is this: some linger for a long time in the ground and some do not. Where possible, prefer the latter to the former. Long lasting, residual weedkillers stop weeds in their tracks but they prevent anything else growing in the soil either.

Glyphosate (Murphy's Tumbleweed or Monsanto's Roundup) is one of the most useful of the non-residual weedkillers. It kills top growth relatively slowly but it works through the leaves of weeds down to the roots, which it also kills. You can use it any time that weeds are growing, though it is most effective when there is the maximum amount of leaf for it to cover. Docks and nettles are best sprayed just as they are coming into flower. (*See also* Weeds.)

Herbs

Earth mothers start here. There is a lot more to herbs than cooking. In the garden, they divide roughly into dry and wet. The dry ones are the Mediterraneans: sage, thyme, rosemary, etc. These need sun and well-drained soil. The wet ones, parsley, mint, chives, angelica must have much damper soil. They will also thrive in half-shade. Herb gardens, which started as apothecaries' dispensaries, are now very vogueish. Before you make one in a prominent place, ask yourself what it will look like from the beginning of July onwards.

Honey Fungus

One of the big bogeymen of gardening. Your neighbour will probably tell you you've got it as soon as you move into your new house. It is a soil-borne parasite that attacks the roots of trees and shrubs, causing slow decay and eventual death. Apple trees, privet, rhododendron and roses are particularly susceptible.

It is very difficult to treat. Take heart from the fact that, like pneumonia, it only finishes off things that are already weak because of some other cause—often drought or old age.

The fungus appears above ground as a honey-coloured toadstool but the damage is done below ground by black bootlace rhizomorphs (*qv*) which invade the roots of the victim. You can best avoid getting it by digging out all old roots of trees or shrubs that you cut down. If you suspect you already have it, you can sterilise the soil with creosote.

Humus

The word comes straight from the Latin, meaning soil or earth. It is what gardeners call the dark, crumbly mixture which results from the breakdown of leaves and other vegetable growth.

The most convenient way to acquire humus is to build a compost heap. You need humus to bind soil particles together and to improve soil structure. As the humus breaks down in the soil it also releases nutrients for the plants above. (*See also* Compost, Loam, Manure, Mulching, Soil.)

Insects

To the gardener, there seem to be more baddies than goodies. There aren't, but the goodies are slower on the uptake and the gardener's patience is limited. Aphids are the most common horrors, the green particularly enjoys roses, the black goes for dahlias and broad beans.

Whiteflies come in two varieties, indoor and outdoor. The indoor one is a menace in greenhouses. It is in artificial environments such as these, often without natural predators, that there is most call for a bottled medicine. Spray plants, particularly *under* the leaves with malathion (pbi's Malathion Greenfly Killer or Murphy's Liquid Malathion) or permethrin (available in many products such as Boots Kill-a-Bug or Bio Long-last).

But remember your friends. Avoid using kill-all sprays that get rid of allies as well as enemies. If greenfly are your problem choose a specific insecticide such as ICI's Rapid, rather than Sybol, based on pirimiphos, which kills every insect in sight.

Your friends are ladybirds, which as adults and larvae eat prodigious numbers of aphids. The larvae are the hungrier and can dispatch about fifty aphids a day each. They are slatey-blue with a few orange spots. Nettles will help ladybirds build up in spring in time for the big rose push. Ladybirds fatten up on nettle aphids.

You should also encourage ichneumon flies, by planting golden rod and fennel. Ichneumons are leggy, four-winged insects which prey on caterpillars. It is not a simple gobbling job. The female fly lays her egg inside a caterpillar and the larva eats its way out from the inside.

Centipedes are excellent predators. Slugs are their preferred diet but they will make do with other pests. Big black ground beetles (get an identification guide—there are 4000 different British beetles) are also keen on slug breakfasts. (*See also* Greenfly, Mealy bug, Pests.)

Insecticides

These should be used with extreme reluctance. In the natural cycle of events, pest build up is followed by a similar build up of predators, but there is a hiccup in the middle when gardeners are most likely to reach for the bottled final solution.

Unnatural imbalances are often caused by predators, such as cats, that we have artificially introduced into the natural chain. In cities, where there are more cats than could star in a million musicals, there are relatively few birds. This has an effect on the food chain.

Insecticides work in several ways. The simplest are those that kill by contact. You spray the bug. It drops down dead. Other insecticides leave a deposit on the leaf which is then eaten by the creature. Caterpillar killers work this way. Systemic insecticides are more devious. These are absorbed by the tissues of the host plant and get into the sap. The insects are killed by eating the plant that you have sprayed. Sap suckers such as greenfly and blackfly are usually tackled this way.

The least dangerous times to spray are early in the morning (say before 10 am) or in the evening (after 6 pm) when there are less beneficial insects on the wing and bees are less likely to be working flowers. Millions of bees, which do no harm to anyone, are killed each year by reckless spraying. Spray when foliage is dry and when there is no wind.

Use insecticides that are as specific as possible to the insects you want to get rid of. Pirimicarb is the ingredient to look out for if you want to get rid of aphids. (*See also* Spraying.)

Intercropping

This is a way of squeezing more produce out of less ground. It will only work if you keep your ground well fed and watered. You need to find complementary crops: one that is faster than the other, or ones that grow in different directions.

Radish is the classic intercropper. It grows fast and you can sow it between rows of carrots or parsnips, for instance, which take much longer to mature. Sweetcorn needs vertical space and the plants are set out quite far apart. Use the space under them for growing trailing marrows or courgettes.

Jealousy

Jealousy is a regrettable trait but rife in the horticultural world. It takes gardeners in different ways. When you are a beginner, you are jealous of the speed and ease with which proper gardeners prune and sow and scuffle earth about with their feet to wonderful effect. This is blameless, however, compared with the far more devious jealousies that arise among seasoned gardeners. This is the dark side of garden visiting, now a national obsession to rival football.

"Well, of course she has a gardener," is one of the deflating phrases you hear as you are admiring an immaculate herbaceous border. Or, "I've never really liked *Salvia leucantha* . . ." Then you watch as the despised salvias shift off the plant stall into the hands of their detractors faster than crockery at a Harrods sale.

Kitchen Garden

In our dreams, this is still a Mr McGregor patch, bounded by old stone walls. Espalier pears spread their arms to the sun and the ground is quartered with neat rows of cabbage and Peter Rabbit's soporific lettuce. The reality is likely to be a shrunken version of this dream. Think of using fruit and vegetables in a decorative way, integrated with the rest of your garden. Use cordon apples to make a screen. Edge patios with parsley, interspersed with viola. Plant an artichoke in the flower bed. Use a standard gooseberry to give height in a patch of annual flowers.

Knowledge

When you have been gardening for half a lifetime, you realise that this commodity is better gleaned from experience than from books but, meanwhile, books provide a necessary lifebelt. Plants will mostly try to grow, whatever you do to them. They will also die, even if you are the world's acknowledged expert on the species. You will learn more by watching the plants themselves than from any other source.

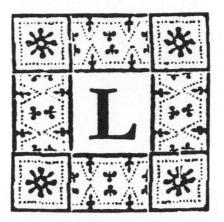

Law

If letters columns are any indication, this seems mostly to do with neighbours. Common complaints are the state of boundary fences and the space taken up by overhanging trees. The law should always be the last resort. Simple bribery with a couple of bottles of wine will prove less aggravating and usually more effective.

On the matter of trees, the law allows you to cut down branches of a neighbour's tree where it is overhanging your boundary, but not an inch beyond. A tree owner recently won damages from a neighbour who had inadvertently cut the offending branches six inches the wrong side of the boundary wall.

You are not legally entitled to any wood you cut

off. You must deliver it to your neighbour, which may only add insult to injury, but that is what the law demands.

Boundaries can only be checked with title deeds and even these may let you down. If no clear owner is marked, the fence or boundary is deemed to belong to the person on whose land the fence posts stand. If that is not you and you want something done, offer to share the cost of renewing the fence. That will not make it yours, but may be better than waking up each morning to a sight that makes you want to scream.

Leaf Mould

Not a disease, but a fine, crumbly specialised type of compost which you make by stacking fallen leaves in a heap on their own. Autumn leaves are far too valuable to be wasted on a bonfire.

The easiest way to make leaf mould is inside a cage made from chicken wire. You will need a space about four feet square (one and a half square metres). If you do not have room for this, pack leaves in plastic dustbin liners instead. The leaves gradually rot down to make an excellent mulch, especially for lime hating plants such as azaleas and rhododendrons. Leaf mould is also valuable as a top dressing for bulbs.

The best leaves to use are those of beech and oak. Leaves with thick midribs, such as ash and horse chestnut, take much longer to rot down. Leaf mould is excellent for improving soil and also provides food for plants. (*See also* Compost.)

Lime

Some plants love it, others curl up their toes at the first touch of it. The plants that hate lime are called calcifuges. These include some of the most popular of spring shrubs such as rhododendrons and pieris. The lime in the soil locks up certain plant foods which they need, to thrive. In the long run, it is better not to struggle to grow lime-haters in limey soil. Although there are corrective medicines such as chelated iron (Sequestrene) which help you to cheat, it is better to go with the flow. Grow what wants to grow and gardening will suddenly seem less problematical.

Loam

This is what good gardeners get when they go to heaven. Loam is perfect soil: neither too wet nor too dry, neither sticky nor sandy. It contains a perfect blend of clay, sand and humus, with just the right amount of mineral seasoning. If you work hard at the leaf mould, you may get loam in the here and now rather than the after.

Machinery

You either love it or you hate it. Either way, beware the attitude that once you have bought the machine you have done the job. Hedge-trimmers need to be given outings, though they are painful to operate. Strimmers need to strim, though the noise is excruciating and the line will keep disappearing up the handle. If you have a lawn, a mower is essential. The need for any other machinery should be carefully evaluated before you buy. Some jobs, such as hedge cutting, are so seasonal that you might find hiring a more economical option. Then if the machine does not work, you can take it back rather than kicking it.

Manure

This is a valuable source of organic matter, which improves the structure of the soil as well as its fertility. In the country, it is easy to get hold of. In the town, you will have to loiter round police and army stables with a large sack. Pigeon lofts are another good source of manure in towns. Like chicken manure, pigeon droppings are high in nitrogen, and dry and light to handle.

Farmyard manure is best used when it has rotted down and looks like Christmas cake. You can use it for mulching roses and other shrubs, and for digging into the soil. This last operation is best done in two stages. Spread the manure on top of the soil during the winter and then dig it in during early spring when it has softened and broken down further. (*See also* Compost, Humus, Mulching, Soil.)

Mealy Bug

This is a tropical pest that attacks house plants and greenhouse crops as diverse as cacti, fuchsias and orchids. It is easy to recognise. The bugs are small and white, and give the impression of being covered with a waxy-looking wool. At all stages —

adult or larvae — they are a nuisance. They feed on plant sap and excrete a sticky liquid which, in turn, attracts sooty moulds. They usually sit round the crown of a plant, tucked into leaf axils, and in other places where it is difficult to dislodge them. In suitably cosy conditions they will breed all year.

The chemical solution is to spray with diazinon (ICI Ant Gun) or malathion (pbi Greenfly Killer, Murphy Liquid Malathion) every two weeks. If they are not too widespread, pick the mealy bugs off with a dry paintbrush or one dipped in methylated spirit.

There is also a biological control, a black and orange Australian ladybird called *Cryrtolaemus montrouzieri*, which eats mealy bugs and lays its eggs inside them. It eats prodigious numbers however and then, if it runs out of that fodder, may start to eat other ladybirds.

M<small>OSS</small>

In Japan they make gardens of it. In Britain we try to strangle it at birth. There is no accounting for taste. Most of those who hate moss hate it most in lawns. You can use moss killers which are based on iron sulphate, but prevention is better than cure. Moss usually appears because a lawn is badly drained, compacted, underfed or choked with thatch, the dead stems of old grasses. On trees and stone, moss looks superb and it would be vandalism to scrape it off. I like it in lawns too. It is luxuriously soft underfoot.

Mulching

A mulch works like a biodegradable blanket; by putting a layer of some sort on the soil you can control weeds, retain moisture, improve soil structure, add nutrients (slowly) and keep plants and crops clean. All mulches are good, but some are better than others.

If you use gravel as a mulch, for instance, you will not expect it to do anything by way of feeding, but it is excellent around alpines. It prevents mud splashing on to low growing flowers and provides efficient drainage around the necks of plants prone to rot in too-damp soil. Gravel is also useful in small herb beds, keeping the foliage clean.

Mulches of materials that have once been plants themselves provide extra nutrients to the soil and also improve its condition, as earthworms gradually pull the mulch underground and aerate the soil. Use compost, manure, hay, straw, leafmould, lawn mowings, shredded bark, mushroom compost, spent hops or seaweed. Each reacts in a slightly different way.

Compost often contains weed seeds, which is a

disadvantage. Lawn mowings are frowned on by some experts, but as our lawn never sees any herbicides, I have no qualms about using them round fruit bushes where they keep down annual weeds.

Mushroom compost is brilliant stuff, easy to use and sterile, but it is slightly over-limed, so is not suitable for a mulch round acid-loving shrubs, such as rhododendrons and azaleas. All mulches should be spread two to four inches (five to ten centimetres) thick if they are to keep down annual weeds. No mulch will prevent the growth of perennial weeds. (*See also* Compost, Humus, Manure, Soil.)

Naturalising

To do this, you grow garden plants in places such as grass or woodland in a way that makes them look natural rather than introduced. To do it successfully, you need to find out what sort of habitats the plants you have in mind would choose for themselves. You also need to choose varieties carefully. The daffodils with the biggest flowers are not the best for naturalising. They also blow over more easily than wild-looking kinds such as the pheasant's eye narcissus.

Bulbs are the easiest plants to naturalise. Plant them in large groups of the same kind, much as a colony might grow up in the wild. Avoid straight rows. The easiest way to do this is to toss handfuls of bulbs on the ground and plant them where they fall.

In light woodland conditions, herbaceous plants such as Solomon's seal and lily of the valley can be naturalised. Blue monkshoods (*Aconitum napellus*), bugle (*Ajuga*), aquilegia, the variegated arum, astrantia, foxgloves, epimediums, *Euphorbia robbiae*, some hostas, pulmonaria and some of the quieter violas can also be naturalised in lightly-shaded situations, provided they are not too dry.

Nettles

Some gardeners consider weeds in the garden to be a sign of moral degeneration, the horticultural equivalent of cockroaches behind the cooker, but there is usually a good reason to keep a few weeds about the place. Nettles, for instance, attract a particularly early aphid, food for the hungry ladybirds waiting for the three-star meals to come later in the season.

Nettles are also an important source of food for the caterpillars of peacock, red admiral and small tortoiseshell butterflies. They can also be turned into a liquid feed. To make this, soak about two pounds of freshly cut nettles in a barrel of water. You can use the liquid straight from the barrel after a couple of weeks.

Organic

This is the most over-worked buzz word in gardening. At its simplest level, organic gardening means working with nature rather than against it. It means gardening without chemically-based pesticides, using fertilizers that you have made yourself (compost) or which have been directly derived from plants or animals (bonemeal).

If you want to go the whole, purist hog, you should join the Henry Doubleday Research Association at the National Centre for Organic Gardening, Ryton-on-Dunsmore, Coventry CV8 3LG (Tel: 01203 303517). You should, anyway, visit it, purist or not. There are always interesting new gardening techniques being tried out there.

Central to the whole business of organic gardening is some understanding of the interdependence of living things. We are the ones rocking the boat, the only ones in the system who now don't understand how we fit in. To be a good gardener, you need respect for living things.

Perennial

This applies to a group of plants, usually herbaceous ones, that unlike annuals and biennials are programmed to exist for more than one or two years. They may not. It depends how well you treat them. Some perennials are more tenacious than others. Lupins are relatively short lived, while acanthus is practically indestructible.

Pests

Novice gardeners will probably get the idea from gardening books that there are an awful lot of them: mangold fly, mustard beetle, pea moth,

rhododendron sawfly, gall mites, leaf blotch eelworm and the like. In mixed plantings, however, there is little likelihood that your garden will be wiped out by any of the above. Bugs exist to feed other creatures. If you annihilate them with insecticide, the predators will go, hungry, elsewhere. Then when the pests come back, they won't have any competition. Aphids are the most common pests, especially the greenfly that congregate on roses. If you cannot bear to wait for order to reassert itself, spray with an insecticide, but choose one that is specific to the job in hand.

Ph

This is a scale which measures the amount of lime that there is in the soil. The scale stretches from 0 to 14, with neutral somewhere in the middle. The "ideal" soil (unless you are a rhododendron buff) is said to be somewhere between 6·5 and 7.

Vegetables do best on a soil that is about 7·5. The letters stand for potential of hydrogen. You can get a rough idea of how your soil measures up with a DIY soil testing kit. Remember to take samples from more than one part of the garden. You can tinker with acid soils, if you want to make them more amenable to vegetable growing, by adding extra lime. It is far more difficult to convert an alkaline soil to a comfortable home for lime-hating plants. (*See also* Acid or Alkaline.)

Planting

Do not plant the pot as well as the contents. There is a certain logic in doing so (plant easier to move if you have made a mistake, roots not disturbed, job quicker and simpler to carry out) but it does nothing for the long-term future of the plant in question. Roots must run.

Make a hole bigger than the one you first thought of and have a bucket of compost standing by. Ease the plant out of the pot, settle it so that the stem sits in relation to the ground at the same level as it was sitting in the pot and work the compost in the bucket round the plant's roots, firming it as you go. Fill in with the soil you took out. Water the plant thoroughly after planting, a drench not a sprinkle. If it is very dry, mulch round it after watering.

Pollination

You need to think about this if you want to grow a lot of fruit. Some fruit trees are self-pollinating, in which case you can expect fruit, even if it is the only tree in the garden. Other trees need help from a neighbour if they are to bear a crop. The pollinator obviously needs to be out in bloom at the same time as the tree it is pollinating. In good catalogues, such as that of Scotts of Merriott in Somerset, fruit trees are numbered, so that you can be sure of picking a matching pair. Morello cherries are self fertile. So is the 'Conference' pear, though it fruits better if it is pollinated by another variety.

The other vital factor in pollination is a good supply of insects. Commercial growers have hives of bees to move into their fruit orchards. Tomato growers release specially bred bumble bees to work in their glasshouses. Bees have suffered appallingly from the thoughtless use of insecticides. Think before you spray.

Pricking Out

When you have got through the first stage of seed sowing (getting the seeds to germinate) you will have to face this second hurdle. You need to give each seedling more room to develop and you do this by transferring them one by one to a seed tray filled with compost. The compost needs to be well firmed down and .the holes roughly two inches apart each way. You can buy boards which will make the holes and firm the compost in one operation. Handle the seedlings only by their leaves, never the stem, which bruises easily. Set the seedlings deeper than they were growing previously. The leaves can sit on the surface of the compost. Keep the seedlings well watered. If you are growing colour-mixed annuals, prick out a mixture of the stronger and the weaker seedlings. The most interesting flowers are often the ones that come from less robust seedlings.

Pruning

The first thing to realize about pruning is that plants do not die without it. There is no ghostly pruner in the wild, flitting about with secateurs to get briar roses into shape or trim up the hawthorn.

Gardeners prune to enhance flowering or fruiting, to create specific foliage or bark effects, or to keep on top of a tree or shrub that wants to be bigger than they want it to be. The second thing to realise is that the diagram in your manual will never look like the plant that is confronting you in the garden. Demonstrations are easier to follow and are held at many centres, such as the Royal Horticultural Society's garden at Wisley, the Northern Horticultural Society's garden at Harlow Carr and at local horticultural colleges. Invest in the best secateurs you can afford.

In any pruning exercise, take account of the shrub's own personality and do not impose your own upon it too vigorously. A garden is not a parade ground.

Quarrels

Who left weedkiller in the watering can? Who mowed over the primroses? Who forgot to open the greenhouse door? These kind of quarrels are easier to get out of the system than more insidious arguments. Can you plant a magenta geranium next to a yellow potentilla? Should there be scillas or grape hyacinths under the *Magnolia stellata*? You could compromise on puschkinias. Or divide and rule over separate areas of the garden.

Rhizome

This looks like a root but is not. It is a stem which has adapted itself to store up food. Roots trail from under it, buds sit on top. Bearded irises have rhizomes which do best sitting on top of the soil where they can be baked by the sun.

Rootstock

You hear a lot about these when you go to buy a fruit tree. A rootstock lends its roots to another plant which, grown on its own roots, would behave differently. Fruit trees are sometimes put on dwarfing rootstocks, which makes them less vigorous. Roses are often grafted on briar rootstocks which makes them more vigorous. The join is made by a graft. Good ones are imperceptible. Bad ones are like a crooked elbow. Sometimes, the rootstock makes a bid to take over the graft. In roses this is called suckering. It happens with flowering cherries too, many of which are grafted on *Prunus avium* roots. The suckers should be cut or pulled out as soon as you see them. Always plant with the join above the level of the soil, otherwise the plant that is grafted may try to make its own roots and the benefit of the rootstock will be lost.

Shade

This is not half as bad as gardeners make out. I much prefer the shady bits of my own garden to the sun spots. Shade is more mysterious, and there are plenty of plants that will thrive there.

Dry shade, between the roots of trees is the most demanding. Feed such ground generously with lashings of compost, leaf mould, and other bulky manures. This will gradually enrich the ground and make it capable of sustaining a greater variety of plants.

In dry shade, *Cyclamen hederifolium* is a star, with flowers of magenta or white in late summer and magnificent marbled foliage for at least nine months of the year. Try brunnera, *Geranium endressii*, ivies and omphalodes, too.

The most difficult sort of shade is that under an evergreen, such as cupressus, but even here, if you attend to the soil properly, you can persuade other plants to grow. Think of lily of the valley, the Gladwyn iris (*Iris foetidissima* with brilliant orange autumn berries) and Solomon's seal. Annual busy lizzies are also tolerant of shade.

Other shady places may be caused, not by overhanging trees, but by the shadows thrown by buildings and boundary walls. These may not be as dry. Here you can grow aquilegia (columbines), bugle, foxgloves, hellebores, hydrangeas, pulmonarias, violets and many types of primrose.

Aristocratic shrubs, such as rhododendrons, also enjoy dappled shade, but to grow these successfully, you need acid soil or a pot filled with ericaceous compost.

Soil

This is a mixture of bits of rock, water and organic matter such as rotted leaves. Sandy soils are made from relatively large bits of rock, clay soils from small particles. One is called light, the other heavy.

Soil needs looking after. This means adding bulky manures to improve soil structure. This extra humus closes up the big spaces in sandy soils and makes it capable of holding more water. In clay soils, humus adds extra air spaces between the too closely-packed particles and so improves drainage.

In town gardens, it is more difficult to acquire bulky manures, but make a resolution to haul in a sack of something nourishing once a week until the whole plot has been covered. It will pay enormous dividends in improved growth.

No amount of chemical fertiliser will change the structure of your soil. Before plants can take up food, they need roots which can find it. Plant roots need passages along which they can run and from which they can then absorb the necessary nutrients for healthy growth. Humus helps to create the passages. (*See also* Humus, Manure, Mulching.)

Sowing

To the uninitiated, seed sowing is the impenetrable rite of passage that separates the novice from the seasoned gardener. Like having babies, it is not usually half as difficult as experts would have you believe. Nor do you need great batteries of equipment. The heat of a propagator may catapult a seed into growth faster than would otherwise happen, but at some stage the plant has to adapt to crueller conditions. A light, warm kitchen window-sill could be the kindergarten of a wide range of flowers and vegetables grown from seed. Use vermiculite to cover seed that you have sown in pots of compost. It is light and retains water at just the right rate.

Spraying

You either do or you don't, and neither party will ever convince the other that they are in the right. I draw the line at insecticides, but use a herbicide (only glyphosate) with enormous gusto. I have persuaded myself that this does not interfere too much with the complex interrelationship of living things in the garden. You can have too many nettles. About bugs, I feel more strongly. I don't want to kill them myself but am delighted if they fulfil their destiny by providing breakfast for a bird. I have never understood, for instance, why tits should be fed with peanuts rather than left to eat the aphid eggs that are part of their natural diet in spring and summer. In winter, too, if it is mild.

Prey is usually a step ahead of predator. You never get enough ladybirds until there are too many aphids, but you learn not to fret. The cavalry catches up in the end, as in all the best films.

If you *do* spray, use equipment that makes the best possible use of the pesticide or herbicide. Most sprayers work by squirting the spray under pressure through a nozzle, which breaks up the liquid, but unevenly. The most efficient sprayers use a spinning disc to regulate the size of droplet needed for any particular target. You use less spray more effectively.

This technique is called Controlled Droplet Application by Micron, who pioneered the technique. More information from them at Three Mills, Bromyard, Herefordshire HR7 4HU (Tel: 01885 482397). (*See also* Herbicide, Insecticide.)

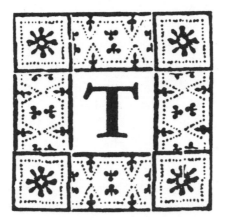

Taxonomy

This is the business of naming plants. Beginners fret and chafe at the amount of Latin that hangs around plants and wonder why the whole lot cannot be jettisoned in favour of plain English. The problem is that plain English will only take you a short way along the road. Take columbine, or granny's bonnet. Excellent names, comfortable names, both of them, but there may come a time when you discover there are several diffcrent sorts. How do you distinguish them? Big, medium and little is too imprecise and does little justice to the magnificent diversity of plant families.

Aquilegia is the proper name for all columbines, its Latin tag. This is called the genus, the bundle that contains all types of aquilegia. The genus is split into different species, each of which has distinct characteristics.

Within the aquilegias you may choose *Aquilegia alpina*, which, as you would guess, comes from Switzerland and is a staggeringly beautiful plant with grey-green leaves and blue and white flowers.

Many species, such as *A. alpina*, are one-offs, just themselves. Others have been seized on by enthusiasts and tinkered with to produce another sub-division in the taxonomony table: varieties. *Aquilegia vulgaris*, being a naturally variable species has been the parent of many named varieties, 'Blue Star', 'Nora Barlow' and at least thirty others.

If you had fallen in love with *A. alpina* however, you would not want to be fobbed off with 'Blue Star'. The only way to be sure of getting what you want is to know a plant's proper name. It is worth the sweat. We care that people should use our names properly. We should treat plants with the same regard.

Tools

A strong and comfortable trowel and hand fork are essential. Pick them up several times to check that they fit the shape of your hand. Stainless steel tools are horribly expensive, but wonderful to use. And good tools will last for ever if you clean them before you put them away and don't leave them out in the rain.

Secateurs are also essential. It pays to get a pair a notch stronger than the norm. I have always used red-handled Felco secateurs and find them faultless. For a biggish garden you also need long-handled loppers, if only to save you busting your secateurs.

A border-sized spade and fork are big enough for most jobs. It is a good idea to save up for stainless steel; although the spade will not keep its edge as well as ordinary steel, the advantages still outweigh the disadvantages.

Demand for powered tools has soared. I am against them (except for lawnmowers) because of the noise they make. Hand shears will cope with anything except a vast amount of hedge and edge. They are also lighter on the shoulders than powered clippers and strimmers.

Aerators, mechanical cultivators, leaf sweepers, rollers and the like are unlikely to be in use enough to justify buying them. Hire instead. If you grow vegetables, you will need a line and a hoe, cloches and a dibber.

Trace Elements

Chemicals in the soil, such as boron, copper, iron, manganese and zinc, are generally lumped together under the heading trace elements. In fertile soil they are present naturally, but lack of them shows up in plant deficiency diseases. Organic animal manures are rich in trace elements and their regular use in the garden should prevent any deficiency problems. Bleaching between the veins of young leaves is sometimes a sign of iron deficiency. You can correct this by using a compound such as Sequestrene made from chelated iron. Magnesium is necessary for plants to produce the chlorophyll without which they cannot live. You sometimes see magnesium deficiency in greenhouse tomatoes that have been treated too liberally with a food high in potash. Leaves turn brown and wither. Correct this with Epsom salts. Magnesium is more likely to be deficient in acid soils than alkaline ones.

Training

This applies chiefly to climbers and fruit trees that you plant as a screen or against walls. Without some form of training, climbers end in a bundled mess under the eaves — or collapse in a heap on the border below.

The point of training is to display the plant to its best advantage and for this you need to bear in mind its natural habit of growth. Butchering is not training, even if it enables you to fit a twenty foot shrub on a ten foot fence.

Clematis for instance is a scrambler by nature. It will always look best wandering through some bulkier host shrub, viburnum or ceanothus or rose. You can enhance the effect by spreading the shoots out in different directions for maximum effect.

You can also persuade climbing roses to do better than average by bending some of the growths outwards towards the horizontal. The tension this creates causes a whole series of flowering shoots to break along the stem, so that you get a better display than you would if you left the rose to its own devices.

The training of fruit trees is a more complicated affair and depends greatly on correct summer pruning of side shoots. A book is vital. Try either *Pruning and Training* by David Joyce (Mitchell Beazley) or *The Essential Pruning Companion* by Professor John Malins (David & Charles).

Transplanting

This entails moving a plant from one home to another with the least possible shock to its system. Summer is the most difficult time to do this, as the plant needs more water than at other seasons. Transplant in the evening, water the plants in thoroughly and continue to water them until they seem to have settled.

The larger the amount of earth clinging to the roots, the quicker the plant will settle, as it will still have a proportion of its fine, feeder roots connected to the soil. This is why it is not worth cramming too many seedlings into a seed tray at pricking out time. It may seem an economy then, but at planting out time it will be difficult to disentangle the roots

Turf

Turfing is an expensive way to make a new lawn, but satisfyingly instant. The best time to lay turves is in October. Then they do not have to struggle against possible drought. As with carpeting, price dictates quality. The cheapest turf is usually the roughest, with coarse grass and no guarantee against weeds. But where children and animals are the chief users of a lawn, it will be wasteful to lash out on turf of bowling green quality.

Turves should be of even thickness (about one and a half inches, four centimetres) and well rooted. Even the cheapest should be free of obvious weeds such as dandelions. They are usually supplied in rolls three feet long by a foot wide and you lay them in rows, staggering the joins as you would brickwork.

Initial preparation of the site is as important with a turfed lawn as it is with a seeded one. The earth on the surface should look like breadcrumbs and you must avoid hollows which may become bogs when it rains.

Unintelligible

This applies to the instructions on any knock-down, DIY piece of equipment which has "Assembled in five minutes" plastered on its packing. Beware. Instructions are always written by people who have done the job a zillion times before and cannot comprehend the panic that overwhelms a first timer confronted with seven pieces of tubing, three bolts and a lost wing nut, all supposed to transmute into a gazebo. Stay simple. Avoid equipment that tells you it packs away flat after use. Unless it is there, up and running you will not use it at all.

Vine Weevil

Its hideous white larvae cause serious damage to plants growing in pots. Peat composts are seventh heaven for them. It will be interesting to see whether they thrive as happily in peat substitutes such as coir. The damage is done by the grubs munching on plant roots. You rarely see the adult weevils as they feed and move at night. The most interesting thing about them is their sex life. Males are extremely rare in the species. Females reproduce without the usual encounter. The most effective chemical control (Aldrin) has been withdrawn, but you can entice adults into rolled-up tubes of corrugated paper. Like earwigs they like resting up in crevices during the day and then

you can have your evil way with them. There is also a non-drying glue (supplied by Agralan) which you can paint round the rim of plant pots to trap the adult weevils. They are crawlers rather than flyers.

Virus

A word abused as much in the plant world as it is in the human. It is a godsend for experts caught on the spot at a gardeners' question time. "Must be a virus", they say when all else fails, and everybody nods sagely, gazing at the wizened leaf in question. Gardeners much prefer to be told that they have got something interesting like a virus than that they are not looking after the shrub properly in terms of aspect, food and drink.

A proper virus is a tiny organism, smaller than a bacteria, which lives and reproduces inside plant cells. Most are pathogens, causing disease in the plant as they are carried about in the plant's sap.

Viruses are spread from plant to plant by sap-sucking insects, most often aphids. Seed from virus-infected plants will not usually carry the virus, but cuttings, or any other vegetatively propagated material will be infected.

The most obvious sign of virus is that plants are distorted, the flowers or leaves streaked and flecked, discoloured or stunted in growth. Occasionally, this is welcomed. The complicated markings on the petals of many highly-prized florists' tulips are caused by virus.

One of the most common viruses is cucumber mosaic virus, which affects herbaceous perennials as well as cucumbers. Leaves grow small and crumpled and are flecked with bright yellow patches.

 atering

Watering gardens is a luxury, not a prerogative. Plants growing in restricted spaces such as pots and hanging baskets need frequent drinks. The rest of a garden should not. Use plenty of organic manures to enhance the water-retaining capacity of the soil. Mulch thickly. Then let nature take its course.

Weeds

You need to know what they look like, especially in their seedling or underground forms. A friend, tackling her first garden in winter, unearthed a warren of bindweed roots, although she did not

know then that that is what they were. After
digging over the ground, she replanted them
tenderly in finely-sifted earth. Their gratitude was
boundless.

On the other hand, if you think a plant is pretty,
keep it, even if know-all friends tell you it is a
weed. Corydalis, the wall weed with ferny leaves
and yellow flowers, is a case in point. Daisies are
enchanting. So is speedwell. Call it by its proper
name, *Veronica*, if it makes you feel better about it.

The worst weeds are perennial ones: bindweed,
marestail, ground elder. They are all supported by
deeply entrenched subterranean networks. Digging
and pulling weakens them eventually. Glyphosate
(as in Monsanto's Roundup) is surer.

Docks and dandelions are well anchored with
long taproots, but once dug up they are done for.
They will resprout if you merely snap them off.
There is immense satisfaction in drawing a large
dock from the ground with all its root intact.

The hoe is the best way of dealing with annual

weeds in the vegetable garden. Sowing seed in rows makes this job easier. Among flowers, I prefer to weed by hand, as there may be interesting self-sown flower seedlings which you want to keep. *Verbena bonariensis*, for instance, can easily be lost to an over enthusiastic hoe. (*See also* Herbicide.)

ild Garden

Despite the image, this may well be the most labour intensive patch of your plot. There is a romantic notion that creating a wild garden is merely a matter of buying a packet of mixed wild flowers (usually heavy on cornflowers and poppies), scattering them to the wind and letting dear Nature take its course.

The chief difficulty is that the showiest wild flowers (poppies, cornflowers) are flowers of the cornfields, flourishing on a regime of yearly tilling and clearing of the ground. After a neck and neck race with the corn, they seed themselves, ready to bob up after the next round of ploughing. Where grass is permanently established, as it will be after the first year of a newly-sown flowery mead, poppies die out. End of vision.

Fertility is another big problem. The best shows of flowers in the wild are where you have poor ground — thin chalk, rocky screes. The flowers zoom up and get the essential business of setting seed over as quickly as possible in the first half of the summer, before food and drink run out. Most garden soil is too good for wild flowers. It encourages the growth of lush grass and rank, leafy weeds such as sow thistle, nettle and dock.

In spring there is a fragile truce and this is when wild gardens are at their best, the turf studded with primroses, violets and, if it is damp, fritillaries. But by mid June, the battle has been lost. Tall grass has its own beauty, but all too often, the whole waving mass is felled by a sudden thunderstorm.

Interest in gardening with wild flowers has increased in direct proportion to the rate at which their natural habitats are disappearing. Instead of creating your own, think about directing some of the time and money it will use up towards saving the rather more successful ones that still exist, though precariously, in the wild.

Finally one has to confront the impossibility of X, Y and Z. The danger with alphabets is that having got to the end, you think you know the lot. With gardening, learning never stops. The more you know, the more you realise you don't know.

Beginners want rules: now is the time to plant out potatoes, this is the way to take cuttings of geraniums, or germinate seeds. Like bringing up babies, this was once information that was absorbed by example rather than swotted up from books. And as in child-rearing, a good model, a personal mentor, is better than any page of words.

Rules are of limited use in gardening. They act as a kind of lifebelt when you are starting off, but they can be deceiving. In the end, a gardener is better served by his own powers of observation. Rules presuppose standard parameters, but vagaries of climate and season and soil mean that the gardener's parameters constantly change.

Do not be bossy with your plants. Watch what they are trying to do and learn from them. Give all things in the garden the benefit of the doubt. One spring you will wake up realising that you are not a beginner any longer. Good luck.